Saving Women and Infants from Abortion

A DANCE IN THE RAIN

Margaret Driscoll and
Emily Faugno

Paulist Press
New York/Mahwah, NJ

Cover & book design by Lynn Else

Library of Congress Cataloging-in-Publication Data

Driscoll, Margaret.
Saving women and infants from abortion : a dance in the rain / Margaret Driscoll and Emily Faugno.
    p. cm.
Includes bibliographical references.
ISBN 0-8091-4393-3 (alk. paper)
1. Abortion—United States. 2. Abortion counseling—United States. 3. Abortion—Religious aspects—Catholic Church. 4. Abortion—Moral and ethical aspects. 5. Pro-life movement—United States. I. Faugno, Emily. II. Title.
HQ767.5.D75 2006
261.8′36—dc22

                                            2006008255

Published by Paulist Press
997 Macarthur Boulevard
Mahwah, New Jersey 07430

www.paulistpress.com

Printed and bound in the
United States of America

Contents

This book has been written for anyone who has ever gone to pray or engage in sidewalk counseling at an abortion mill, anyone who is seriously considering it, and all who prayerfully support this vital work. May you find encouragement here.

Both authors have agreed that all profits from the sale of this book will be donated to the Helpers of God's Precious Infants.

Preface
Msgr. James P. Lisante

Among the great tragedies connected with abortion is the fact that its direct and immediate victims are without a voice for themselves. Most others who suffer injustice may be robbed of their voices, but they do have them, and they may eventually be able to speak up on their own behalf.

Unborn children in the womb are literally without voices of their own. In considering abortion, their natural defenders—their mothers and fathers—have chosen to ignore these new human lives and have decided to treat them as less than human inconveniences, or even as threats to their own happiness and well-being.

No doubt some pregnancies arise in seriously difficult circumstances. Deeply troubled mothers and fathers in panic and fear can persuade themselves that they have no alternative to abortion. Who is to speak on behalf of the children alive within the womb and to explain the value of these lives even in the most difficult and trying of circumstances?

This book tells the story of those who are willing to be the voices of the voiceless, of people who have such hope, faith, and love that they are willing to speak up, even in the face of what would seem to be the most hopeless situation of all—the moment when a woman is actually about to enter an abortion clinic.

Surely at that point a woman has made up her mind and is unlikely to be persuaded otherwise. But the Helpers of God's Precious Infants believe that where there's life, there's hope. They know that as silent as the child in the womb may be, that child still speaks a message to his or her mother. That message is that each and every child, whatever may be the circumstances of the child's conception, is a unique and irreplaceable gift from God.

These sidewalk counselors speak the words that make this silent message of the child resound in the parents' ears so that they are challenged to rethink the decision for abortion, whether it is tentative or seemingly firm. And, praise God, in many cases, as the reader of this book will see, that is exactly what happens as the message of life conquers the lure of death.

The Helpers of God's Precious Infants do not rely only on their own powers of persuasion; they rightly rely even more strongly on the power of prayer that God himself will inspire the change of heart in those who are about to choose abortion. Things impossible to humans are not impossible to God, for whom all things are possible. And God's Holy Spirit can soften the hard heart and cause those to hear who have been deaf even to the most eloquent of human appeals.

The women who are urged to choose life over abortion are offered assistance by the Helpers of God's

Precious Infants that is both spiritual and also very practical, so that they can cope with a pregnancy that may be surrounded by very difficult circumstances.

So often has the pro-life movement been criticized by its opponents as being interested in the lives of the unborn only up to their birth, that it is important to emphasize that those who struggle on behalf of the unborn also assist mothers and children after birth. And even women who choose abortion are offered assistance, through a program called *Project Rachel,* to deal with the deleterious emotional impact the abortion has had on them.

This book gives the reader in living detail the experience of offering the challenge of choosing life to those about to choose abortion. The reader will see how tentative this decision often is and how it can be turned around by the witness of one other person to the value of life.

Looked at from the point of view of the millions of abortions that have been performed in this country in the last thirty years, the question is, "But what can *I* do?" Looked at from the point of view of the unique value of each human life, the question really ought to be, "How can I afford *not* to do something?" And what person would not be rightly proud to say, even once, "I saved a life today"?

Prologue

The Rain—Price Tags on Children

College degree, high school diploma,	*> a child's life*
A new job, a promotion, job security,	*> a child's life*
A new home, a new car,	*> a child's life*
Reputation, public opinion,	*> a child's life*

The father of the child is married	
to someone else,	*therefore a child must die.*
The father wants the child	
aborted,	*therefore a child must die.*
The relationship with the	
father has ended,	*therefore a child must die.*
I'm too old to have another child,	*therefore a child must die.*
I'm too young to have a child,	*therefore a child must die.*
My husband is unemployed,	*therefore a child must die.*
I lost my job,	*therefore a child must die.*
The father of the child is out	
partying all the time,	*therefore a child must die.*
I already have all the children I want,	*therefore a child must die.*
I just had a baby,	*therefore a child must die.*

Saving Women and Infants from Abortion

Our present culture has misdirected so many into thinking that legal abortion enhances a woman's freedom. The truth is that a postabortive woman carries a deep emotional and spiritual wound from the experience always.

When it's raining shades are drawn, streets are quiet, doors are closed. Not many want to be out in the rain. Some put in an old movie, snuggle up on their couch, and wait for the rain to go away. And some curse the rain. They say it is depressing, that you can't see clearly where you are going, and it seems as though it will never stop. Perhaps they are tempted to go out in the rain, but find themselves too busy with other responsibilities such as work, cleaning the house, taking care of family, cooking, repairs, and so forth.

Our culture at times seems dark and rainy. We continue to deny the existence of our younger brothers and sisters, and the scourge of abortion hovers over our spiritual, emotional, physical, and psychological lives like a rain cloud threatening our survival.

In 1997, 1.33 million abortions took place in the United States. Women aged twenty to twenty-four obtained 32 percent of these abortions.[1] According to the Alan Guttmacher Institute, black women are more than three times as likely as white women to have an abortion, and Hispanic women are roughly two times as likely. Fifty-eight percent of women having abortions in 1995 had used a contraceptive method during the month they became pregnant.[2]

According to the New York State Department of Health, in 1999 there were 132,681 abortions in New

York State. The abortions in New York City accounted for 95,981 of this total. During 1999, Nassau County, on Long Island, New York, suffered 4,205 abortions, and 5,980 abortions were obtained in Long Island's Suffolk County.[3] In 1999, 119,179 live births and, as stated above, 95,981 abortions took place in New York City.

These numbers are overwhelming. As if you were caught in a rainstorm, you can easily get discouraged and stay inside, immobilized, waiting for the rain to stop, waiting for our norms to change.

We are surrounded with raindrops of despair, atheism, agnosticism, selfishness, deception, and apathy. Why dance underneath all these raindrops? Why not be busy with sunnier skies? Mother Teresa of Calcutta reminded us that we are called not to be successful but to be faithful. When we are faithful, success is not far behind.

It continues to rain in our world, in our church, and within our very selves. Many are intimidated by the torrents of the Culture of Death; they stay inside, afraid of getting wet. But there is a small group of people all over the world who have come out into the rain. With the light of life, they have braved the floods and begun dancing in the stillness of the cities. Their sun dance is drying up the raindrops one at a time by reaching out with God's love to bring about conversion of hearts. They are members of the Helpers of God's Precious Infants.

The Helpers of God's Precious Infants pray for and speak to the men and women who come to the abortion clinics. Offering temporal and spiritual assistance, they are often heard by those in need. The Helpers may be the only voice to speak what these individuals coming to the abortion clinic believe deep inside: that their child is a gift from God and is wanted. The Helpers recognize the little ones in the wombs of their mothers as brothers and sisters; they welcome these children into the human family and embrace them spiritually. The Helpers pray for these children and support them with prayer should their lives be taken away.[4]

The following chapters are a meditation on the rain in our world, the rain in the church, and the rain within. The dance is a response to the rain, and the turnaround stories offer hope for the Culture of Life yet to be fulfilled.

Notes

1. See Alan Guttmacher Institute/ Research Arm of For Profit Planned Parenthood website at http://www.agi-usa.org.

2. Ibid., 2.

3. See New York State Vital Statistics website at http://www.health.state.ny.us/nysdoh.

4. See Helpers of God's Precious Infants website: http://members.aol.com/infants1/aboutus.htm.

CHAPTER ONE

The Rain in the World

With every child that is born under no matter what the circumstances, the potentiality of the human race is born again.

James Agee

~ *1* ~

The Rain—Too Many Have Died

Millions of children in our country have been killed in their mother's womb.

The Dance—The Business of Love

"The fact is that some choices have victims, and when somebody's choice destroys somebody else's life, that's everybody's business. It is, after all, the business of love to intervene to save our brothers and sisters in need."

—Father Frank A. Pavone, Priests for Life

Hope for the Culture of Life

The Red coats came

Sometimes it is the pictures in the brochures that teach. Our pamphlets have pictures, factual and in color, showing the step-by-step development at all stages of the fetus in the womb, as well as photographs showing how abortion mutilates and destroys. Some women refuse to look, hoping to erase the reality of what they plan to do. But sometimes these pictures can literally be lifesavers.

Two attractive women arrive, so similar in looks and height, wearing identical red coats, that one could easily assume they are sisters. But no, one is the pregnant daughter seeking abortion, the other her brokenhearted mother absolutely against it. The daughter walks right past me into the clinic while the mother stops to talk.

"I do not want to be here," she says vehemently. "This is wrong, but my daughter will not listen."

In her twenties, the daughter lives with a girlfriend and is pregnant by a married man with two children. She does not want to break up his marriage, but neither does she want to have a child without a father. To her way of thinking, there is only one solution: get rid of the child.

The mother continues, "I took her to a priest but she would not listen. I have room for her and her child in my home, but she has made up her mind. I am here because I cannot abandon my child. But right after this I am going to church."

With only a few seconds to make my case, I thrust our best, explicit, factual pictures into the hands of this distraught mother. "Show these to your daughter," I implore.

An hour later, mother and daughter emerge from the clinic smiling, totally transformed. The daughter has decided to keep her child.

"What changed her mind?" I ask.

"It was those pictures you gave us," the relieved mother replies.

After hugs all around, those two red coats, fusing into one, sway in unison, as arm in arm, once more at peace, mother and daughter walk away with their baby safe and sound.

What a beautiful picture they make! "Yes, it's true," I say to myself, "a picture is worth a thousand words." In more ways than one!

Helpful daughter

It may also happen that a daughter helps her mother. Both mother, age thirty-nine, and daughter, seventeen, accept the literature offered, as I mistakenly suppose it is the daughter planning to have an abortion.

Even if it is wintertime and cold as it is this day, many escape the crowded ugliness of the waiting room, as does this pair, by stepping outside for a few minutes.

It gives us a chance to speak to the people, as I do to this mother who is crying, and her concerned daughter.

With two children, ages seventeen and ten, this mother does not want to start with a baby all over again. The husband agrees. As we discuss the situation, it is the daughter who shows the mother that she is wrong, the daughter who promises to help, the daughter who is generous enough to accept and welcome a new baby brother or sister. A teenager with a head on her shoulders!

"You're lucky," I tell the mother. "This baby will keep you young. You have the chance to start all over again, with a wonderful daughter to help you."

Moved by her daughter's love, the mother embraces the new life within her. Together they go home, a united family once again, with a brand new member on the way.

~ *2* ~

The Rain—Should I Care?

Who really cares if these people have abortions? They already have too many children on public assistance. Someone should sterilize them. Why do they need so many children?

4

The Dance—Who Gets to Live?

The above sentiment is eugenics at its best (or perhaps its worst). This mentality is adolescent yet common. Public assistance is an investment in the future. It exists more for the children than for the adults. We will always have the poor with us, and we will be judged according to how we treat them. In December 2002, it was announced that there were more than 38,000 homeless people living in New York City. This is the highest number ever recorded. "There but for the grace of God go you and I," said St. Vincent de Paul. Your gifts, whether material or spiritual, are gifts from God. You are accountable for them.

Are we the same people who say children are our hope for the future?

Pope Paul VI explained responsible parenthood in *Humanae Vitae*. A couple should only have the number of children they plan on being responsible for and in grave circumstances should use natural family planning. This is to cooperate with God. The sterilization mentality is in direct contradiction with God and is bound to end in a complete disaster.

Let's think about this eugenics [sterilization] attitude. Here are ten possible reasons our society could enact (involuntary) sterilization laws:

1. They already have too many children.
2. They are on public assistance.
3. They are mentally challenged.

4. They are_____(*you fill in the ethnic group*), and we already have too many of them in the community.
5. They can not possibly afford another child.
6. They did not graduate from high school.
7. They did not graduate from college.
8. They have a criminal record.
9. They are terminally ill.
10. They are immigrants.

Who is going to decide which of these should apply? Should we have a majority vote? I suppose it's all fine and good if we don't fall into one of these categories, but chances are we fall into one or more of these categories. Are there any volunteers to be sterilized?

How far a jump is it from (involuntary) sterilization laws to forced abortion? In December 2002 a *New York Post* columnist wrote, in an article in which she was expressing her frustration with the welfare system, "It's a woman's choice to have a child. Why should the city and state and working taxpayers support the child you had but can't afford?"[1] As mentioned earlier, the Alan Guttmacher Institute's research claims that 58 percent of women having abortions in 1995 had used a contraceptive method during the month they became pregnant.[2]

I suppose the biggest complaint among the so-called middle class is that the poor are having too many children on public assistance. Why does that bother them so? There will always be some who fall through the cracks. It's a tough world out there. What do they have against them? Do we really know where our tax money is going?

Poor people may not be slick like some in the middle class. Can we say that we have never been assisted by the public? Are we sure? Never fudged on our taxes? How about when our parents went into the nursing home? Ever transfer any funds? How much? $200,000? $300,000? $1,000,000? That money would feed a lot of hungry people. It is more than a family of eight would get over a ten-year period from public assistance.

We say: "My parents worked hard for their money; that family of eight didn't. My parents should not have to give their money to the government. They are entitled to free nursing home care." But who's supposed to pay for it? What does it cost for one person in a nursing home per year? $80,000? $100,000? Who's going to pay this cost? Probably the eight kids who grew up on public assistance, made it through the tough times, and have been working and paying taxes for the last fifteen years.

Yes, those who advocate sterilization may be intellectually sophisticated, educated, and civilized, but they are morally blinded from the mist of the rain.

Hope for the Culture of Life

The Lady she wore around her neck

Sometimes one can feel incredulous, annoyed, and yes, even downright angry at such irresponsibility: he is married to someone else, has three children; she has three children of her own, and now, together, another is on the way—or is supposed to be. He, at least, does not want the baby aborted, argues, loses the battle, and leaves. She goes into the clinic with a woman friend. Since each one has refused our pamphlet, I wait to speak to the friend, who soon comes out to smoke.

Although she has tried to discourage this abortion, she has failed. I notice a gold-colored miraculous medal on a chain around her neck.

"Catholic?" I ask.

"No, Baptist."

Surprised, because most Baptists do not wear medals or use rosary beads, I inquire, "Do you know you are wearing a miraculous medal, a medal of Mary, the Blessed Mother of God?"

"I don't know who or what this is. Someone gave it to me, so I wear it."

"Do you know anything about our Blessed Mother at all?"

"No."

"Did you ever hear about Jesus' first miracle, the wedding feast at Cana? How when there was no more wine, Mary told her Son, Jesus, and he changed water into wine just because she asked him to?" (I had to do this fast!)

She hadn't heard that story.

"I think Mary is very pleased that you are wearing her medal, and you belong to her in a special way. I'm sure that if you ask her she will help you persuade your friend to keep her baby."

The friend didn't truly understand, but she went back inside anyway to try again. I wish I could have been in on all the conversations: the friend asking Mary, who tells Jesus, who speaks to the heart of this woman who is about to enter the killing area. The communication must have been good, because soon the two women come out—one still with her baby, the other with her new mother, Mary.

Blue

She stood with her back against the mailbox, separate from the crowd, just waiting quietly for the doors to open.

Sometimes the best way to open a conversation is to offer a rosary. Which I do—a bright blue one.

She refuses it, saying, "I'm not going in there for 'that.'"

"Please take this rosary for your baby."

"I don't have a baby."

"Will you take it for a future baby? It matches your bright blue earrings. It belongs to you."

Reluctantly she accepts the rosary as the doors open to welcome her inside the clinic. "Our Lady of the Rosary, please help her," I pray.

Later, as quietly as she walked in, she walks out. "I came out because I respect what you are doing," is all she says. And then she goes home as quietly as she came—but differently. Because of blue earrings, a blue rosary, and most of all because of a special Lady traditionally pictured dressed in blue.

Mary is her name

There really isn't much for me to do. The friend who accompanies Sheila doesn't want her to do it. The boyfriend, not present but in contact by phone, persistently calls to urge Sheila not to do it. And then, the way she shies away from me as I attempt to give her a pamphlet is a giveaway. She is afraid to look at anything that might change the course of events, abortion being the event!

However, while the nausea of pregnancy is ever present (and that is what she really wants to be rid of), Sheila's three little boys at home have already honed her into a loving, responsible mother. Her resolve to abort starts to weaken, and she comes out.

Learning of her three boys, I hand Sheila a rosary and ask, "Don't you think it's time for a baby girl?"

"I guess I would like a girl," she muses, smiling at the thought.

As she starts to walk away, she stops, turns around and, looking at me intently, inquires, "If it's a girl, what should I call her?"

I have never been asked that question before, but I didn't have to reflect on it even for a second. Without hesitation I reply, "*Mary* is her name."

How real is Sheila's baby now, how much already loved, because this baby has a name. It is *Mary*, the most beautiful of all names. I pray that Mary, Mother of God, may watch over her newest namesake, Baby Mary, and Sheila, her mom.

~ *3* ~

The Rain—The Price of a Soul

Politics, politics, politics…

Sometimes one wonders which corporation owns the seat in the White House, and other times it just seems obvious.

On January 23, 1993, the *Times Union* of Albany, New York, reports:

"President Clinton marked the 20th anniversary of the Supreme Court's Roe vs. Wade ruling Friday by dismantling a series of Reagan and Bush administration restrictions on abortions." His executive orders came only hours after the annual Right to Life March was held. By executive order, Clinton

- ended a five-year ban on fetal tissue research;
- overturned the so-called gag rule that restricted abortion counseling at 4,000 federally funded family planning clinics nationwide;
- acted to revoke prohibitions on the importation of RU 486—known as the French "abortion pill";
- allowed abortions at U.S. military hospitals overseas;
- reversed a 1984 order, known as the "Mexico

City policy," that prevented the United States from providing foreign aid to foreign organizations that perform or promote abortion.[3]

The Dance—The Culture of Life

On January 23, 2003, *Newsday* (New York City) reports:

"On the 30th anniversary of the Supreme Court decision that legalized abortion, President George W. Bush yesterday told a large anti-abortion rally that he shares with them 'a commitment to building a culture of life in America.'"

He called on all Americans to "protect the lives of innocent children waiting to be born." The president continued: "For thirty years, the March for Life has been sustained by constant prayers and abiding hope, that one day every child will be born into a family that loves that child and a nation that protects that child... and when that day arrives, you will have the gratitude of millions—especially those who know the gift of life because you cared and kept the faith."[4]

Hope for the Culture of Life

Infection, anyone?

It had been an extremely hot, uncomfortable summer, and how I had longed for autumn with its invigorating, snappy, energy-producing coolness. But now, in early November, we are having unusually chilly, wintry days, and I'm not yet used to it. I had forgotten that with cold weather comes a problem for sidewalk counselors: we experience stiff, unfeeling, unyielding, numb frozen fingers that have difficulty distributing or even holding our pro-life pamphlets (gloves notwithstanding!).

A friendly young woman, Carole, age twenty-seven, mother of four children and ready to enter the clinic, says she doesn't need a pamphlet because:

"I'm just going in for a checkup."

"To see if you're pregnant?"

"Yes."

"And then what?"

"And then I'll decide whether to have an abortion or not. I really don't want or need a fifth child. It won't take long for a blood test and a sonogram. I'll be out soon."

Sensing that she can be persuaded not to have an abortion, I keep my eye out for her. But two hours pass and still no Carole. I fear the worst because no exam should be so time-consuming. Finally she appears.

"My exam took so long because I have an infection in my body. I have to take antibiotics and can't have an abortion until the infection leaves and I am perfectly healthy."

"So, what does this mean to us?" I ask, using a schoolmarm's approach.

"I guess it means that God has put a roadblock in my plans and I shouldn't have this abortion. Well, not now anyway."

"Not ever, agreed?" I correct her.

13

Thinking it over, she agrees, "Yes, not ever."

We hug, and I say: "Now go home, be happy with your five children."

She does, she goes, and yes, we know she will be happy with her husband and family of five.

Did not God intervene at just the right time? He uses anything and everything to save his children—this mother and her baby. He even makes infections useful!

And so, if you and I are subject to "an injurious invasion of body tissue by disease-producing organisms" (dictionary definition for *infection*), let us use this condition to our advantage—and a baby's. The next time we come down with the flu, a cold, or minor illness, and experience the accompanying discomfort and aches and pains, let us offer up this distress for a special baby that is in danger of being aborted that day. If Carole's infection saved a baby, so, too, can ours.

My baby is alive

A polite, doe-eyed, serious young woman enters the abortion mill, soon comes out, and waits pensively by the curb for her husband to take her home in their car.

Only three weeks pregnant, she is instructed to come back in two weeks to be checked again before an abortion can be scheduled.

I am glad her husband is slow arriving. It gives us time to share with her our thoughts and beliefs.

"I have a three-year-old child and a nine-months-old baby. It's just too soon to have another one," Anna confides.

"Are you Muslim?" I ask, noting her dark eyes and distinctive apparel.

"Yes," she admits, "but still I must do this even if it is forbidden."

"And your husband, what does he want?"

"He says that if it is alive, we cannot do it."

"There is no 'if.' Your baby is alive and has been from the moment of conception."

Out comes all the detailed information and pictures to prove my point. As we examine the material together, we note that at three weeks this tiny human being is only one-tenth of an inch long. However, he or she already has the beginnings of eyes, a spinal chord, a nervous system, intestines, a stomach, and lungs. And pumping more confidently now is the primitive heart, which began beating at about eighteen days. Standing close together, we marvel at God's perfect creation.

When her husband arrives and Anna gets into the car, I ask,

"You won't be coming back, will you?"

"No, I know now that my baby is truly alive—even at three weeks."

~ 4 ~

The Rain—Partial-birth Abortion

"In a partial-birth abortion, the abortionist pulls the baby's feet, arms, and shoulders from the uterus and then stops within inches of a complete delivery. With only the baby's head in the uterus, he forces a blunt, curved Metzenbaum scissors into the base of the skull. The scissors are spread to enlarge the opening. A suction catheter now evacuates the skull contents. The baby is then fully removed. This procedure is performed at twenty weeks' gestation and beyond."

—Carol Everett, former abortion clinic owner

When asked during an interview if partial-birth abortion would ever be done for the health of a mother, Ms. Everett said: "Realizing that the partial-birth abortion is a three-day procedure, two days for the dilation and one for the procedure, I believe everyone understands that if the woman's life were truly at risk, the physician would do an emergency C-section. This procedure would save the mother's life and perhaps the baby's life." [5]

The Dance—Turning of Hearts

There are Helpers who have taken early retirement, and others who go to counsel and pray at the abortion mills in the early mornings before going to work. These

Helpers are very instrumental in turning the hearts of women in the later stages of pregnancy. Luminaria (used to dilate the cervix) is usually inserted on a Tuesday, Wednesday, or Thursday. By the time the women arrive on Saturday their hearts may change, but it is difficult for them to become intellectually convinced that they can still try to save this life once the luminaria has been inserted.

Hope for the Culture of Life

A child waiting to happen

I have never seen so distraught a woman as the one who emerged from the clinic one early Saturday morning. Sobbing hysterically, arms flailing wildly every which way and in all directions, she was totally beside herself.

"This can't be. How can this be?" the woman exclaims and questions at the same time, over and over again, as I accompany her down one long block, cross the street, and walk down the next block until we come to a ledge where I persuade her to rest. Married and in her early thirties with a two-year-old child, Rhonda finds herself three months pregnant and she just doesn't want this baby.

"This should not be. I take birth control pills and my husband uses protection. So, how can this happen? We're not irresponsible people. We are very careful. We both work and it's just not time for another baby. Besides, I have this two-year-old 'tyrant' at home and that's enough. *I don't want this baby.*"

She is still upset mentally and her stomach upset physically, so I leave her alone for just one minute to buy her a ginger ale at a nearby stand. I guess I shouldn't have, because when I return a woman passerby has stopped to calm the agitated Rhonda. Of the same race and age and also the mother of a two-year-old, these two women have much in common. I become the outsider as the woman speaks to Rhonda of her own two abortions and Rhonda's "right to choose."

After thirty minutes of trying and making no headway, I return to my post at the clinic door, knowing that Rhonda will have to confront me one more time before going in. Upon her return she ignores me, goes inside, but restless and unsure of herself, she comes out again. We walk again. We talk again.

"What good does it do to call yourself 'Pentecostal' if you won't call upon the Holy Spirit to give you the wisdom and the strength you need right now to overcome this temptation to destroy your baby? At three months of pregnancy your baby is fully formed. She just has to grow. Ask to view the sonogram and see for yourself."

That's what she did and that's when she changed.

"I'm keeping my baby," she decided, as she called her husband to come and take her home. It would be a forty-five-minute wait, and I was concerned about this woman—couldn't let her out of my sight—although one could visibly see her change of heart.

What an obstacle course this baby has had to traverse so far, with so many stop signs along the way. Pills, chemicals, contraceptive devices, and even abortion itself are nothing to this little slugger.

"I'm coming anyway," this young one insists.

"I guess this is going to be one strong, positive child," Rhonda ponders aloud.

"Another tyrant?" I ask, smiling.

Rhonda smiles back, "I can handle it now."

An awakening

Old enough, capable-looking enough, gracious enough to accept our literature and even to stop to speak—I wondered why this couple had come. Maybe just for a routine checkup or a pregnancy test, I hoped. It is important to know why.

It is really difficult to plunge into the intimate, prying questions as soon as one begins a conversation with strangers; but there is no other way, for in a few seconds the couple will be beyond our reach. Hoping that the Holy Spirit will guide us, we must dive in, as prudently as we can.

The gentleman seemed friendly enough, so I asked, "Are you considering abortion?"

He evaded my question, saying, "Ask her." Turning to the woman, as discreetly as possible I inquired, "Why do you think you must abort your child?"

Her polite reply was an astonishing "I really don't know." Dumbfounded by her answer, I continued, "How many weeks pregnant are you?"

"Fourteen weeks."

There wasn't time to plumb the depths of their thinking. "Were they even thinking at all?" I wondered. Do they realize what they are doing? Do they know what a fourteen-weeks-old fetus looks like? I showed them the pictures and text (all documented by scientific research) explaining the week-by-week development of the "young one." By day twenty-one the heart begins to beat; by day forty there are brain waves. By the eighth week everything is then present that will be found in a fully developed adult. By week twelve the fetus sleeps, awakens, opens and closes its mouth, and by week thirteen fine hair has begun to grow. She even sucks her thumb!

What was impelling this couple to reject their gift from God for no apparent reason? Has aborting one's child become just the fashionable thing to do? If the pro-choice counselor inside the clinic is able to influence this couple more effectively than I, then the baby will be lost. Prayer is now my only recourse.

After what seems like an interminable length of time, the couple comes out, having finally decided against abortion. My heart is grateful as together we walk away from the place of death. The parents have awakened in time; the pre-born is safe and sound asleep; and I am walking on air!

~ *5* ~

The Rain—Deception

At the age of seventeen she begins to take birth control pills prescribed by the abortion provider.

Within the next five years she will abort a child at twelve weeks' gestation, have a child out of wedlock, and begin to take depo-provera birth control shots given every three months to prevent fertilization.

At age twenty-four she suffers severe side-effects from taking depo-provera and has an abortion provider insert an IUD. The IUD perforates her uterine wall and ends up in her intestine. This young woman finds herself wondering how she bought into the years of deception that have destroyed her self-esteem.

The Dance—The Spirituality of the Helpers of God's Precious Infants

The Helpers follow a Marian spirituality that patterns itself after Mary, Mother of Jesus, at the foot of the cross. Msgr. Philip Reilly, founder and executive director of the Helpers, states that the Helpers exist both to make sure there is a presence in prayer of God's people at the sites where the unborn are unjustly dying, and as sidewalk counselors who provide help at these same sites to the distressed mothers coming there for abortions.

"The reason the mothers who abort are touched by the presence of God is due to the fact that there is no one present to them in their pregnancy. They feel alone, unloved and uncared for. If they had someone to be with them, they would not kill. When you experience the loving presence of another to you [the Helpers], it gives you life."

—Fr. Michael Minton,
Helpers of God's Precious Infants,
Sydney, Australia

Hope for the Culture of Life

Jump-start for life

When a quiet, respectful young girl with bewildered-looking eyes behind silver-rimmed glasses steps out of the clinic, I can't imagine she's there for an abortion. It's got to be someone else! So fearfully I ask:

"Do you have a friend in there considering abortion?"

"Not a friend. It's my mother!"

Tara, age fourteen, the oldest of three children, has a father who goes to work and a mother who goes to school. Without fully comprehending what is happening, Tara accepts her mom's decision to abort her six-week-old unborn child and dutifully accompanies her mother to the clinic. I ask Tara about her religious faith.

"I don't have any."

"And your mom?"

"She doesn't follow any religion either."

"But you do understand that this is killing your baby brother or sister?"

No answer. And then, "I just came out to get something to eat," she explains defensively.

"Tara, we don't have time for that right now. I have some very important information that I'd like you to bring inside for your mom to read. It will help her to understand how vital it is for her to keep this baby, and how terrible, how appalling it will be if she destroys her child—your very own brother or sister. I want you to understand how special and valuable your role is here today. You alone can help save your baby brother or sister."

"All right, I'll eat later," Tara agrees as she takes all the pro-life material I hand her and goes inside.

Time passes. No Tara, no mom. And then, at 11:00 a.m., when it's time to leave, I see Tara walking up the block.

"Where is your mom?"

"She's down there in the parking lot by our car with the hood up. She can't start the car."

"I guess I missed you coming out of the clinic. Did your mom have the abortion?"

"No, she changed her mind. She's keeping the baby."

I hug Tara. "What a wonderful big sister you are. This little boy or girl will always be very special to you because you helped save its life. I'm so glad you're going home."

"Well, we can't go home because we can't start the car."

Coming down to earth, and hoping he has the proper equipment, I ask John, a pray-er, and a man one can count on in any emergency, to jump-start the car. He immediately drives down to the parking lot, assesses the situation, and with a little coaxing, the car springs into action.

While John is busy with the car, I congratulate the mom. As several prayer group members gather around us, I introduce my young friend, Tara.

"Oh, Tara," joyfully explains Patricia, a pray-er, "you're the one we've been especially praying for all morning—you and your mom."

Tara looks from Patricia, to John, to me, and to the entire group, each in his own way wanting to help.

"Who are these people who care about us?" the still-puzzled Tara is probably asking her mom, as with a burst of energy the car leaves for home with a more confident mom and a blissfully unaware, unborn baby.

Tara, we are the Helpers of God's Precious Infants—some of whom pray, some of whom counsel, one of whom fixes cars. The Helpers—who jump in to save babies just starting to live. Teamwork at its best!

The prayer that binds us

Every Saturday evening, winter and summer, you'll find me attending the 5:00 p.m. Mass—this time in the basement because the church is being renovated.

It is damp and rather uncomfortable as, to the annoying tune of whirring fans, we sit on unyielding metal folding chairs. None of us is sitting in his or her accustomed place and I find myself positioned next to my friend, Maryanne, who grabs my hand in prayer for the recitation of the Our Father.

As we pray the familiar words I am no longer in this makeshift atmosphere, but standing on the sidewalk outside of an abortion mill. Delia, a young seventeen-year-old mother of a one-and-a-half-year-old girl, has come with her own mother, Kim, to have an abortion. Kim is the mother of ten children, and Delia is her youngest. Never having had an abortion, Kim is happy that she has accepted all the children God has sent her.

But Delia is different. "I'm only seventeen, already saddled with one child, have broken up with the baby's father, and I have to go to school," she protests. Yet, she accepts our leaflet as she enters the clinic.

In time, leaving Delia inside, Kim comes out, saying, "She's reading it, and it's bothering her."

When Delia, still determined to have this abortion, comes out looking for her mother, we continue our conversation.

"Are you Christian?" I ask.

"No, Baptist."

"Then you *are* a Christian, just as I am a Christian, being Catholic. Do you know the Lord's Prayer? May we pray it together?" I inquire as she allows me to take her hand.

She knows every word—I do not have to prompt her—as we beseech the Lord to "lead us not into temptation, but deliver us from evil."

This feeling, however, doesn't last long.

"I'm still doing it," she declares defiantly, "even if it's wrong."

Kim watches her youngest go back inside, torn for this daughter for whom she can now do nothing more, nor can I. But the Lord can. Just as I am leaving to go home, Delia and Kim come out.

"We're going home for now, but I may still come back," warns Delia.

"I don't think so," I counter, "not if we continue to pray the prayer that binds all Christians together; not if we continue to ask Our Father to deliver us from evil."

Now each time I attend Mass and hold hands and pray the Our Father, I remember Delia and pray for her and for all the Delias in the world.

~ 6 ~

The Rain—Rejecting Children

"Radical Feminism has become the cutting edge of individualism. We are in the midst of a unilateral rejection of children, and there are signs all around that children are not the most important thing in the world to someone."

—Elizabeth Fox-Genovese,
Syracuse, New York, March 27, 2004

The Dance—A Distinct Role

"Pregnancy, childbirth, and motherhood are distinct to women. A woman's relationship to her children is integral to her sense of self and well-being. We need confidence to be faithful without being apologetic or rigid."

—Elizabeth Fox-Genovese,
Syracuse, New York, March 27, 2004

Hope for the Culture of Life

The tools of our trade

After invoking the Holy Spirit for guidance, and after prayer, our most important equipment, our most powerful weapons against abortion are our leaflets, pamphlets, and brochures. As we speak with the abortion seekers we try to tailor these pamphlets to their individual needs.

When a young man escorts a young woman into the clinic, leaves her there, and comes out, I am glad if he is willing to stop and explain their situation.

"Cathy is my sister and she won't change her mind. She's twenty years old—a grown woman—has two kids already, the boyfriend has disappeared, and she doesn't want and can't afford this baby. I don't want her to do this, but…"

"Here then," I interrupt, "bring these pamphlets inside to Cathy. They will help her change her mind."

27

"No, I can't do that. She won't read them and they will be wasted."

"Just one then, just this one. Have her read *just this one*," I wheedle, as I press a small leaflet into his unwilling hand.

When they come out a short while later I am surprised. I am amazed. The girl seems taller and straighter as she holds her head high. There is a spring to her step, a smile on her lips, and a pride in her demeanor that wasn't there before.

The reason? It has to be the leaflet—the only one I could coerce the brother to give Cathy, entitled "The Most Important Person on Earth." It reads:

> "The most important person on earth is a mother. She cannot claim the honor of having built Notre Dame Cathedral. She need not. She has built something more magnificent than any cathedral—a dwelling for an immortal soul, the tiny perfection of her baby's body.
>
> "The Angels have not been blessed with such a grace. They cannot share in God's creative miracle to bring new Saints to Heaven. Only a human mother can. Mothers are closer to God the Creator than any other creatures. God joins forces with mothers in performing this act of creation…
>
> "What on God's good earth is more glorious than this: to be a mother!"
>
> —Joseph Cardinal Mindszenty

Taking these words to heart, Cathy now knows that she herself is a cathedral housing a tiny new human being; she is a temple for its immortal soul. Is it any wonder that she is walking tall?

Is it any wonder I feel my bulging, awkward, heavy, pro-life material–filled bag suddenly becoming weightless? I am struck anew by the force of our literature— the tools of our trade.

A Christmas story

It is five days before Christmas. As each abortion seeker approaches the clinic I hand out a flyer, and in keeping with the season, exhort, "Please keep your Christmas baby. It is a Christmas gift from God."

Three couples heed these remarks and accept their God-given Christmas gifts. Three Christmas babies are now safely on their way to being born next summer.

Having been sidewalk counseling for four hours and feeling satisfied with these three turnarounds, I prepare to leave for home and resume my responsibilities there.

But, just at this point, a couple arrives with a small child, walks calmly and confidently toward the beckoning clinic door, and is about to enter. So intent on leaving am I that it is only as an afterthought that I give the woman a pamphlet—this blue pamphlet that often changes everything.

Her reaction to the leaflet is startling. Without even examining its contents, this emotionally charged woman sobs loudly, hysterically, convulsively. She trembles and shakes violently. Tears fall copiously. She looks ill. In this sad state, there being no way I can talk to her (I'm rather frightened myself), I draw her gently away from the door, hold her close, and whisper as soothingly as I can, over and over again,

"You don't have to do this. We can help you."

The boyfriend, totally confused and perplexed, tries to take her hand but she snatches it away. "Is he the culprit? Is he forcing her to do this?" I wonder to myself.

Turning to him, I warn, "Don't make her do this. She really doesn't want to."

"I'll take care of her," he assures me, as with his arm around her he leads her away, still clutching the blue pamphlet, as they walk up the block.

When I am offered a ride home, I accept. As we proceed slowly up the street I see the woman, emotions now under control, walking back toward the clinic. I want to get out of the car, speak with her again, and help her, but my responsibilities are calling me home.

How could I know then that after reading our blue brochure and studying the pictures of aborted fetuses, she decides to keep her baby and is looking for me to thank me?

It isn't until evening that a series of phone calls puts me in touch with the woman, Barbara. (Patricia, a Helper, having remained behind, learns of Barbara's wish to contact me, takes Barbara's phone number and relays it to me. I immediately call Barbara.)

"I came back to the clinic to find you, to thank you for having saved me from doing that terrible thing, but you were gone. I'm so happy to keep my baby. I'm so glad I can thank you."

"Barbara, I really don't think you wanted to destroy your baby. Was it your boyfriend's idea?"

"No, I was the one. I was having problems and would really have gone through with it if you hadn't stopped me. When my child saw how sad I was not to find you, she tried to comfort me. She said, "Maybe it was an angel who came down to help you, and then she just flew away."

My eyes filled up. Here I thought I was giving Jesus a birthday present. Instead, it was Jesus who gave a Christmas gift to me. Yes, he does things like that!

Notes

1. Johanna Huden, "Pushing People onto Welfare," *New York Post,* December 13, 2002, 41.

2. See Alan Guttmacher Institute/ Research Arm of For Profit Planned Parenthood Website at http://www.agi-usa.org.

3. Karen Tumulty and Marlene Cimons, "Clinton Lifts Curbs on Abortion," *Times Union,* Albany, NY, Saturday, January 23, 1993; reprint from the *Los Angeles Times.*

4. William Douglas, "Protesting Roe v. Wade: Bush Calls for 'Culture of Life,'" *Newsday,* January 23, 2003.

5. Carol Everett, "Partial Birth Abortion; Inches from Infanticide," Easton Publishing Company, Inc., P.O. Box 1064, Jefferson City, MO 65102-1064.

CHAPTER TWO

The Rain in the Church

In the U.S., Catholic women are 29% more likely than Protestants to have an abortion.[1]

It is impossible to further the common good without acknowledging and defending the right to life, upon which all the other inalienable rights of individuals are founded and from which they develop.

Pope John Paul II[2]

We need to bring the Gospel of life to the heart of every man and woman and to make it penetrate every part of society.

Pope John Paul II[3]

~ 1 ~

The Rain—Silence

Silence is complicity.

In 1998, there were 23,943 abortions in Queens County, New York.[4]

According to an Alan Guttmacher Institute study, Catholic women obtain 32 percent of U.S. abortions.

In 1998, Catholic women obtained 7,662 abortions in Queens County.

There are 102 Catholic parishes in Queens County.

In 1998, there were seventy-five fewer children to baptize in my parish.

Silence is complicity.

The Dance—Response

Every month people from the diocese of Brooklyn join their bishop at a local abortion mill. Countless mothers, fathers, children, religious, and single men and women set aside their plans for one Saturday every month and offer up their sacrifices for the families that come to the abortion mills.

Their prayerful voices are not only heard by those who are entering the abortion mill, but also by those already inside. Knowing that God's people are praying for them, women choose life, and their sorrowful hearts find joy again. It is a proven fact, and all sidewalk counselors can testify to this truth: the more prayers we have, the more women turn around and choose life.

Hope for the Culture of Life

Yes, God is here!

The sun, somewhere high above me, seemed not to want to show its face this damp, dreary, and gray early October morning at the abortion mill. But the despicable display below, on the sidewalk, was even less to my liking. The scattered remains of a drinking party lay before me; they included thirteen completely empty beer bottles (Heineken—imported!), some of which were broken, and remnants of food mixed in with dirty rubbish and trash. Six gray-black pigeons roamed studiously about, circling the area—and me—as they greedily picked at this unexpected, filthy feast. The offensive stench of stale beer pervaded the air and hung low over this garbage dump at the entrance to the clinic. This area outside is a mirror perfectly reflecting the sordidness of the activities taking place behind the scenes of the abortion mill door.

Trying to ignore this God-forsaken place, I lift my mind above the refuse, forget the plump and ravenous birds hovering about, and begin my work—prayer—in between handing out pamphlets.

"God," I ask. "Where are you?" "Can you really be here with us?" I question as I pick my way through the rubble.

Soon a woman steps out of the clinic. She declines the offered rosary and refuses to stop and talk, wanting only to get out of here and go home.

Struggling to keep up with her, I ask breathlessly, "Just tell me this: Did you change your mind?"

For a minute, she stops to answer.

"No, I didn't change my mind. *God changed it for me.*"

Yes, God *is* here. And God had been here all the while.

What a dummy am I! I needed this "turnaround" to remind me, and to give me a lesson in faith: no place is God-forsaken if we are open to God's presence, God's voice, and God's love.

Candles

When an electric company truck parks near the corner down the block from "Choices," a woman steps out, walks toward the clinic, accepts our literature, smiles shyly, and goes inside.

Somehow I feel that she won't last very long in there. She doesn't. She soon appears and seems to be relieved when I approach.

"I'm not sure about what to do," explains Monica. "I'm just not comfortable doing this and neither is my husband. We have a twenty-two-months-old daughter who stays with a friend while my husband and I work for the electric company. One child is hard enough, but two?" she asks shaking her head negatively.

"Shake the dust from this deadly place and go home," I advise biblically.

Her hesitant steps need a gentle nudge as I walk with Monica back to the truck. She wants and needs me to convince her that this is the only thing to do—keep her baby.

As we speak about the wonder of new life, I see her confidence return, and her expression of awe at what is happening within her gives a lift to her voice and a lift to our feet. The pallid dim light of her wavering conscience suddenly is afire with a new resolve. Strangers just minutes ago, we are immersed in the same rosy glow and enjoy the warmth that comes from sharing the light of faith.

And then I remember the words of Jesus in Matthew 5:14–16:

"You are the light of the world....Nor do they light a lamp and then put it under a bushel basket; it is set on a lampstand, where it gives light to all in the house. Just so, your light must shine before others..." HERE.

That's what the sidewalk prayers and counselors try to do. It is an honor to be a candle. Sometimes we may flicker in the wind, or be dampened by the rain, but we can never be snuffed out!

~ *2* ~

The Rain—Rejected by Your Own

Maybe your pastor has just denied the bishop permission to lead a prayer vigil from your parish to the local abortion mill. He says there are too many events going on that day in the church (too many activities to do inside). Is this true? Does he really mean that he does not agree with public witness (dancing in the rain)?

Of course he's pro-life! Isn't he? You feel as if you are occasionally thrown a bone by one of the priests in your parish. They may say during a homily: "We as Catholics believe in the consistent life ethic from the moment of conception till the moment of natural death." I wonder if perhaps they are thinking: "There, I said I was pro-life (sort of), but I didn't mention the *A* word, so no one should be offended, and those people who pray at the abortion mills will be happy."

The Dance

God gave you the gift of wisdom. It is one of your greatest gifts and also one of your greatest crosses. Father: "…forgive us our trespasses as we forgive those who trespass against us…." For the times I said things I shouldn't have or failed to speak when I should have. For the things I've done and failed to do, Father forgive me. Let us too understand that just as we are not perfect, neither are our priests. So we continue to pray for them and to dance. Hopefully they will hear us dancing and join in. Approach them continually and invite them to join in the dance.

Throughout your life's journey you may have been fortunate enough to find a couple of individuals who helped you and guided you along the way. At some point in your journey, you must stop looking for leaders and become one. Stop looking for the priests to lead you. If you are blessed to have the knowledge of life, then lead them.

Hope for the Culture of Life

The long way around

It was 7:20 a.m. one summer Saturday, and as three young girls waited for the clinic doors to open, they sat on the hood of their car as we spoke. They were friendly and open as one said, "My two friends and I came up from North Carolina last night for me to get this abortion."

When I expressed astonishment that they would travel such a distance (the clinic is in New York City), she explained, "I used to live around here and I know this place. I have a two-year-old, a one-year-old, and now this one. I'm not married. I realize that this pregnancy is the result of lust, not love, that this shouldn't be, but…"

"You know that this is wrong," lectured one of the friends. Quickly, I gave our literature to the friend, knowing that she would have to be the minister, the priest, the counselor once inside the clinic waiting room.

She did an excellent job. In a short while the three girls came out, and said, "Listening to you has changed our minds. We're going back home to North Carolina."

It may seem that they had made the long trip for nothing. But sometimes we have to go the long way around to arrive at true understanding.

Morning sickness prayer:
"Deliver us from evil"

What a misnomer in her case! For it wasn't just in the morning. It was all day and all night, every single day and every single night. It was nausea without end.

Pregnant for almost fifteen weeks, she couldn't eat, couldn't hold anything down, couldn't take care of her two children or her husband, couldn't take IT anymore. She wanted OUT. She wanted BABY out!

So a very reluctant and troubled husband brings his wife inside for an abortion, and then steps outside to talk. He tells me how tired he is, how worried he is, how he has tried unsuccessfully to talk his wife out of this abortion.

"Why didn't YOU stop her from going in?" he asks in an accusing, fault-finding voice.

"Is this my fault?" I ask myself in alarm. "What are the words that could have helped her, words that I did not say?" But, I'm not here to argue. Instead I plead, "Let's pray."

I take his wet, sweaty, tear-soaked hand in mine and together we pray, as he repeats after me the only words I know, to the only Person I know who can change a heart, the words of the Lord's Prayer.

We say it as earnestly and as confidently as we can, this stranger and I, and then ask God to melt his wife's heart, to quiet her fears, to quell her queasy stomach, to assure her that this is only a temporary, even natural condition that would soon pass.

If these prayers have any effect whatsoever on this wife we cannot detect it, for the husband comes out dejected and defeated.

"Keep praying." I beg encouragingly.

"It's not doing any good," he replies.

We wait. Finally she comes out, crying, "They won't do it. They say I'm too far along."

Too far along? Can't be. This clinic performs abortions through the sixth month of pregnancy. At fifteen weeks, this woman is well within the time limit. Husband consoles wife as he and I smile in surprise. We are certain that neither my words nor his have brought about this astonishing turn of events.

Whose words then? The words Jesus taught us in the Lord's Prayer "...deliver us from evil"? Are these the words that stayed the hands of the abortionist from performing his deadly deed?

And then I realize that while we had been praying for conversion in *her* heart, perhaps Jesus had changed the killing doctor's heart instead. So I learn: God uses us all, in sometimes the most unorthodox, unexplainable ways, and with the most unlikely, unexpected people, and that sometimes we must *pray*, and then get out of God's *way*.

~ 3 ~

The Rain—Outcast

You met a fellow parishioner on the bus once, and he told you about his activities in the parish working with the sports program, and so on. You told him how you awoke at 5:30 a.m. on Saturday to pray at the abortion mill, but it was worth it, you tell him, because you helped save five lives. He has a puzzled look, almost one of shock. "You do *that*?" he asks. The next time you see him on the bus he again speaks of his parish activities— parish council, and so on. You remain silent. You don't feel that you can explain your ministry to fellow parishioners. It's uncomfortable, it's awkward, it's unaccepted.

The Dance—Calvary

God wants us to go to the place where children are dying and women are being exploited. It's Calvary, the place where innocent blood is being shed. To understand why we go to Golgotha, we have to look to Christ. Jesus was motivated to go to Golgotha by the love he had for those who were going to kill him. He wanted the salvation of their souls. They were enslaved in an incredible darkness, and Christ wanted them to be free. The price of their freedom was our Savior's blood.

The lost children of Christ had to experience the love of God. A God who loved his enemies, and forgave them as they were putting him to death. When the people experienced his love, it was then that they truly converted. The thief believed he was a king, and the centurion believed he was the Son of God.

The Risen Christ wants to save the people today who are enslaved in the darkness of the Culture of Death, where innocent blood is being shed. Christ asks us for permission to live within us, and for us to live within God, a communion. Christ then asks us for further permission to go once again to Golgotha through us and in us, his mystical body, the church, the people of God.

We go to bring Christ's truth, forgiveness, and love to a world that is broken and in need of redemption. If the lost children of God see in us the face of Love, the face of Christ, they will believe and their hearts will be converted. It's only when they really meet Christ and his Love and Truth that they will abandon the Culture of Death and embrace the Culture of Life.

John and Mary teach us how to be present at Golgotha. They do not condemn the people there; rather, they are victims with Christ. They are living martyrs. John and Mary did not shed blood in martyrdom later in life. It is what happens within that causes martyrdom. The other apostles who did not make it to the foot of the cross deeply regretted not being present, and would have given their right arms to have been there. But God gave them another opportunity to stand at the cross, and each in his turn paid witness to Christ.

Now it's our turn to stand at the cross, and if you are already at the cross praying and counseling, *do not* feel sorry for yourself. Years from now, people will give their right arms to say that they were outside when women and children were in danger, and people inside were enslaved in the Culture of Death yearning to be free when you brought them the light.

—Paraphrased from Msgr. Philip Reilly,
founder of the Helpers of God's Precious Infants

Hope for the Culture of Life

The fair-haired couple (persistence)

Here's a turnaround wherein I was first ignored, then tolerated, then screamed at, and then finally accepted.

An attractive, tall, fair-haired couple ignores the pamphlet I offer and goes into the clinic. Soon the man comes out and walks down the block.

"May I walk with you?" I venture. "You must know that abortion is a very serious sin. Why do you think you have to do this?"

"There are circumstances, sometimes, and one has to do these things," he explains.

"I don't know your circumstances, sir, but I can see that you are young and strong and healthy, and thus you can do anything. You don't need to step over a dead baby to accomplish your goals."

The man waves me away as he continues to walk down the block. I knew that last statement had been a bit strong and had hit a nerve. Soon he returns and I optimistically walk down to meet him, to try again—only more gently this time. I don't get the opportunity, however, for by now he is very angry and upset.

"Get away from me. Don't come near me. I don't want to talk to you," he bellows.

I step aside (very quickly); he goes back into the clinic.

A while later he comes out with his tall, beautiful, blonde wife or girlfriend. While her eyes look down, his

43

eyes are searching for mine. He wants me to know. Very gravely, very somberly, very seriously, very simply he says the words a sidewalk counselor most wants to hear: WE DIDN'T DO IT!

As I congratulate them, the tall blonde stands silently, her eyes still averting mine. "I'm so happy I want to give you a kiss," I tell the girl. She smiles. She bends her head. I kiss her cheek, and the three of them go home.

As I watch them walk away, I realize that I will never see this couple again. I do not even know their names. Yet, they have touched me and I have touched them to an incomprehensible degree. And for certain, this child has already touched—softly, imperceptibly, yet indelibly—the hearts of his or her parents.

The dark-haired couple

Two weeks later a dark-haired couple goes into the clinic. The man comes out and allows me to walk with him. A security guard making $7.00 an hour, he has an apartment with rent of $750.00 per month. With three children already, there just isn't money or room for this fourth baby.

"I don't want to do this, but…" He stops and sighs hopelessly. I give him five pairs of rosary beads: one for himself, three for his three children, and one for the new baby.

As he goes away for coffee, I return to my post near the door. Presently a pleasant woman comes out to smoke. Says she is married, has three children, no money for this fourth baby, and must get this abortion. I give her three pairs of rosary beads for her three children. When the man comes back and shares a cigarette with this woman, I then realize they are husband and wife as they go back inside together.

I say to Mary C. (another sidewalk counselor), "Look at that! I just wasted eight pairs of rosary beads on that couple." In her quiet way, Mary answers comfortingly, "You never know."

A while later, out they come. They seem happy with their decision, content, at peace. The man looks at me, smiles and, fully extending his arms, states with a simultaneous mixture of victory and resignation—and loudly (he doesn't care who hears him):

"Yeah, yeah, yeah, OKAY, *LADY*, We Didn't Do It!!!"

Eight pairs of rosary beads are a small price to pay for one live baby, Mary C. and I agree. With each rosary we give away, we wish to remind the prospective parents that Mary, our Mother, will always come to our aid if we ask her.

Notes

1. See Alan Guttmacher Institute/ Research Arm of For Profit Planned Parenthood Website at http://www.agi-usa.org.

2. Pope John Paul II, *Evangelium Vitae*, 101, *Origins*, Vol. 24, no. 42, April 6, 1995.

3. Ibid., 80.

4. See New York State Department of Health's Website at http://ww.health.state.ny.us/nysdoh/vs98/table23.htm.

CHAPTER THREE
The Rain Within

"Why do you care so much?" the man asked, looking at me quizzically as we stood on the sidewalk outside of a busy abortion clinic. While doing my best to help this man understand for himself the horror of what he planned to do, his wife called from the clinic door. He went to her side and they both went inside before I had a chance to answer his question.

"Well, sir, maybe it's because this is how you and I began, within the wombs of our mothers. No one forced us out before our time or suffocated us, or vacuumed us out, or burned us with salt, or tore us limb from limb and then threw us in the garbage.

"Maybe it's because I ask, 'If we kill our children, what and where will be our future?' and then I know the answer: 'Our future will be hell—here and hereafter.'

"And because, sir, no maybe about it, if I don't try to do something to stop abortion—then I AM JUST AS GUILTY AS YOU ARE."

~ *1* ~

The Rain—Imposition

Agnostics: I believe abortion is wrong, but I do not want to impose my morality on others.

The Dance—The Gift of Knowledge

"Rescue those who are unjustly sentenced to death; don't stand back and let them die. Don't try to disclaim responsibility by saying you didn't know about it. For God, who knows all hearts, knows yours, and he knows you knew! And he will reward everyone according to his deeds."

—See Proverbs 24:11–12

Hope for the Culture of Life

Thank you

Not remembering if they had even accepted our pamphlet, I see them come out—this young couple. They face me squarely, smile wanly yet courageously, and then, with a voice hardly above a whisper, the girl utters simply the most eloquent of words: "Thank you."

So much feeling and meaning in those two small words—for this couple and for me. She is twenty. He is eighteen, not married, no money to spare, both in college, a hopeful, unobstructed life view ahead—all changed so irrevocably by the positive verdict: PREGNANT.

How tempting to destroy this obstruction, this microchild, and then limp home with no one the wiser *except themselves*.

They couldn't do it. No one had to preach, or cajole, or argue with them. Not one word. Our presence and the vocal responses of the prayer group gave them the resolve they needed to walk away from the greatest temptation they will ever have to face. Satan, this time you LOSE!

Can I ever forget their haunting, heartbreaking "thank you," which for me will reverberate down through the years? Will this couple ever hear my heart-felt "thank you" echoing back to them for their glowing, firm example of faith?

Oh, how I hope so!

The necessary jolt

They are here again, and early, this couple who had come to the clinic last week. They had ignored me then and they ignore me now, so it doesn't look promising. Since I can't intrude or force myself on them (not yet, any-way), I must keep my distance and watch them go inside.

When the woman comes out alone with a cigarette in hand, I approach cautiously. Now she seems ready to talk.

"We couldn't get this abortion last week because of a mix-up with my insurance. Now it's straightened out. Look, we have six kids between us. I have a seventeen-year-old girl with one man, and three kids with my former husband. My boyfriend has two of his own. That's enough."

"Does your seventeen-year-old know you're here?"

"Yes, and she supports my decision."

"Is this what you would want for her if positions were reversed?"

"Yes, and even though we're Catholic, I would stand behind her."

She throws down her cigarette, steps on it to show that the subject is closed, and goes back inside.

Then it's the boyfriend's turn to step outside. I try the gentle approach with him, too, hoping that one-on-one will encourage him to speak. I need not have worried. Whereas before this man was silent and aloof, now I can't keep him quiet. Every pent-up thought and emotion comes to the surface and seeks to be verbalized.

"I've never been happy one day in my life. Why should I bring another person into the world to be just as unhappy?

"I'm Hispanic and discriminated against. My wife has left with our two children, and I don't know where they are. One child is retarded and needs special help. My mother never wanted me, never loved me, and to this day doesn't want to see me.

"I had little education and no guidance at all. I do plumbing work, but only take jobs when I get paid off the books, because I don't want to pay taxes.

"A small child ran into my car—it's not my fault. Now my insurance rates have gone up. Why do these things happen to me?

"What kind of a God is it who allows so much hardship, pain, and unhappiness?"

I listen patiently to his litany of woes as he takes all his frustrations out on this poor little unborn baby. But time is a-wasting and I have to start him off in a new life-giving direction.

"I believe everything you say, and I'm sorry. But nothing, *nothing* that has happened to you is as bad as what you intend to do right now. You plan to kill your child. Can anything be worse than that? Are you not a murderer?"

I had to jolt him, shake him somehow! And jolt him those words did because soon, with tears in his eyes, he brings his girlfriend out.

We don't speak. They have had enough of "irritating" me. I walk with them to their beat-up, dirty white car, wave a congratulatory and grateful goodbye, and hope.

With this one right act, maybe it will help put to rest all the wrong thinking on both their parts. Maybe the mother will go home to teach her seventeen-year-old daughter the value of life. Maybe the man will resolve to be a better parent than his own had been. Maybe this turnaround baby will, by his very newness, make life new again for this couple.

I stick an imaginary, optimistic feather in my light blue cap as I set it straight on my head and go back to my post at the door. My thoughts and prayers remain with this couple now and for a long time to come. It's all part of the job, for they are part of me.

~ *2* ~

The Rain—Fear

"It's really great that you go to the abortion mill to pray. I would go, but I would get too angry. I would go, but it's too early. I would go, but I don't feel well. I have health problems. I would go, but…"

The Dance—Grace

"…a soul in the state of grace has nothing to fear from demons who are cowards, capable of fleeing before the gaze of a little child…."

—St. Thérèse of Lisieux[1]

"…I understood, too, there were many degrees of perfection and each soul was free to respond to the advances of Our Lord, to do little or much for Him, in a word, to choose among the sacrifices he was asking…." —St. Thérèse of Lisieux[2]

"To be happy is to be united to the Sovereign Good…." —Rev. J. N. Grou, SJ[3]

"Neither must we allege our weakness, and say, I never could do this or that, even though grace should demand it of me. The will of God renders possible whatever it commands, because it always joins to the command the means of accomplishing it. God would be unjust if, when wishing us to do something, he did not give us sufficient assistance to do it, since of ourselves we can do nothing….Be not, therefore, dismayed; what appears to you today absolutely impracticable will seem to you, if not easy, at least very possible, when the time for action comes....The usual cause of these reserves is that, seeing before us the vast career of sanctity, and consulting only our present strength, we judge ourselves incapable of continuing to the end."

—Rev. J. N. Grou, SJ[4]

"...God, who is rich in mercy and who never suffers himself to be outdone in generosity, devotes himself, if I may be allowed to say so, to the man who is devoted to him; he treats him as his child, he takes care of him as 'the apple of his eye'" (see Zech 2:8).

—Rev. J. N. Grou, SJ[5]

Hope for the Culture of Life

The frozen zone

For a time the police enforced a frozen-zone policy whereby the counselors could not stand or walk in a certain area near the doors of the clinic. This was difficult for us because men and women often came out for a breather and stood in that zone, and we could now not approach them.

One morning a man and woman entered the clinic. The man, wearing dark glasses and earphones, comes out and stands in the frozen zone directly opposite me. He stands there for a long time but I am not allowed to speak with him. Because of the dark glasses I don't even realize he is looking at me. It seems as if his eyes and ears are blocking out the whole miserable place. All I can do is pray.

Finally he goes back inside, comes out with the woman, and they walk out of the frozen zone. I dart after them, catch up with them, and breathlessly encounter them. Yes, they have changed their minds.

Says the man, "I was watching you standing there all that time, praying. I knew that abortion was wrong but I was afraid to come over to you."

"I was watching you, too," I answer excitedly, "but because you were in the frozen zone I couldn't come over to you."

Now I know that even a frozen zone can't get in the way of God's grace.

Best friend—conscience

They enter the clinic together—Dorothy to have an abortion, and Frances her friend accompanying her.

When Dorothy comes out to smoke she explains, "I have four children with my live-in boyfriend and am now pregnant by another man. This baby has to go." One mistake after another...but this baby *must* live. Dorothy refuses to consider this, and goes back inside.

When Frances takes her turn outside she speaks quietly, seriously, wearily, "I have tried to talk her out of this but she won't listen."

"Right now you are the most important person in the whole world. Neither pope nor president can go in there to talk to your friend, but you can. Only you.

Please give these pro-life articles to Dorothy and try again."

When both women come out smiling, I congratulate them.

"Yes, I'm keeping my baby," says Dorothy resolutely.

"What about your mixed-up home life?"

"I haven't figured that out yet, but my baby stays."

"What made you change your mind on abortion?"

"She did," pointing to Frances, her loyal friend.

"Good work," I say to Frances, as we share a secret smile.

Her fine-tuned conscience, her strong sense of right and wrong could not be silenced. She had to speak her piece one more time, for the sake of peace in her soul. Frances, the friend, accomplished what I, the stranger, could not.

Conscience is a terrible, wonderful thing. It confronts us with difficult decisions and then commands us to do what is right.

Conscience, then, is our best friend. As Frances is to Dorothy.

~ *3* ~

The Rain—Apathy

Summer homes, baseball, basketball, golf, boating, movies, tennis, swimming, gardening, sleep, and so on.

The Dance—The Value of a Child's Life

It is a proven fact that the greater the number of people who come to pray at the abortion mill, the greater the number of turnarounds we have.

Yes, you work hard each day, and you deserve a break. However, we are in a moral crisis. This question is posed: "What would you be willing to give up to save a child's life?"

Would you be willing to give up a day at the beach to save a child's life?

Would you be willing to give up a day on your boat to save a child's life?

Would you be willing to give up a day at the golf course to save a child's life?

Would you be willing to give up a day at the pool to save a child's life?

Would you be willing to give up a weekend fishing trip to save a child's life?

Would you be willing to give up a weekend skiing trip to save a child's life?

Would you be willing to give up a baseball game to save a child's life?

Would you be willing to give up a day at the mall to save a child's life?

Would you be willing to give up a day of rest to save a child's life?

Would you be willing to give up a day working in your garden to save a child's life?

Would you be willing to give up a trip to the park or the zoo to save a child's life?

Building the Culture of Life takes sacrifice. You are part of a movement. You are changing the world one life at a time. No recreational activity will spiritually rebuild you like sidewalk counseling. God will not be outdone in generosity. Try it and watch what good things God will bring to your life.

Hope for the Culture of Life

Morning glory

When a young woman arrives at the clinic at 7:00 a.m. on a Saturday and the doors don't open until 7:30, she is usually determined to get an abortion, even if she tells you that she is just there for a pregnancy test.

Enid was polite and accepted our literature and my conversation, but I was skeptical when she told me that a pregnancy test was all she was there for. She also insisted that, if pregnant, she would keep her baby. I hoped it was true; she seemed like such a lovely girl.

I was really happy when a long time later Enid emerged smiling, indeed pregnant and glad to be so. Not only that, she had shared our literature with another woman (who had refused to accept it from me) as they sat in the waiting room. Upon reading our pamphlet, the second woman changed her mind, decided not to have the abortion, and left with her baby close to her heart.

As Enid stood on the sidewalk close to the prayer group, waiting for her boyfriend to pick her up—a half-hour wait, at least—I suggested she rest on a bench a short distance away. But she declined. "I want to stand here and listen to the people praying. Their prayers and songs are beautiful and comforting and I'm enjoying them very much."

Not only did Enid assist in the turnaround of a stranger, but she appreciated our prayer group, too. How fortunate for me to have arrived early and to have made the acquaintance of this flower, this "morning glory" of hope and good cheer.

Only sixteen

The sky is overcast, gloomy, and gray. *Dismal* is the word for this day in late July. A number of women, some crying, all sorrowful, have already come out, their abortions having been completed. All are emphatically sure that they will never do this again. After giving each a rosary, a Rachel's Helpers leaflet, and information where they can go for help, I watch sadly as they depart.

And then comes Jenny. Jenny is sixteen, African American, sweet, very pretty, and all alone. She is frightened but determined to end the five-week-old existence within her.

"My father is a doctor; my mother is a nurse; my brothers and sisters, all older than I, have gone on to college and made something of themselves. I'm only sixteen and still have two more years of high school to complete. I can't tell my parents. They will kill me. My boyfriend, who is seventeen, does not want this abortion, but I am African American, he is Caucasian, and his family doesn't like me. I have no choice. I will bring shame down on my whole family. I am Christian. I go to church every Saturday night, and I hate to do this but there is no way out. I'm only sixteen."

This story, as old as creation itself, is new again in Jenny. Although we encourage her strongly to let us take her to the nearest crisis pregnancy center to talk it all out, and to see her situation as hopeful, Jenny refuses. "I'm sorry, but this must be done."

And yet, fifteen minutes later, still crying, she comes out. "I'm going to do it. I'm just not going to do it today."

A start in the right direction, but the real work has just begun.

Our jobs have just begun. We must pray for all the Jennies of the world. Because the Jennies keep coming, day in and day out.

As kind and sympathetic as we wish to be, the truth must be told. Jenny didn't follow the rules and admonitions of the Good Book. It couldn't happen to me, she thought, "I'm only sixteen."

An understanding family can help her now.

And prayer.

For the sun should shine on sixteen-year-old girls.

Postscript: The following Saturday a woman came to the abortion mill and told us that Jenny had told her mother, who was accepting of the new life. Jenny was keeping her baby, and was okay.

Just be there

It is mid-February, temperature in the twenties, at 7:30 a.m. At my post only fifteen minutes, with three and a half hours to go, already I am feeling the cold.

"Oh, God," I advise him, "I'll stand here and shiver and shake and suffer, but don't expect me to speak persuasively or convince anyone not to kill her baby. My face is so stiff and frozen that I can't even move my lips to talk. I am so heavily clothed that all I can do is waddle slowly toward the people as they approach. I won't be able to do a good job today. You will just have to take over."

"Go to work, anyway," God seems to insist.

So I give out pamphlets, force a smile, and feebly attempt to waylay the abortion seekers who pay no attention, who only want to get in out of the cold.

"This is impossible," I tell myself negatively. And yet I argue, "I'll soon be home where there will be warmth, and food, and comfort, and acceptance. It's where I belong. But most of the babies who come here are only in temporary housing. Their mothers only reluctantly give them food, and warmth, and shelter, and then desert them—to be tortured and evicted from their rightful home. So how, then, can I not be here, ineffectual as I may feel?

My musings are interrupted by a young woman who exits the clinic.

"I didn't do it because my I.D. card isn't right. Maybe it's not to be. I guess maybe I'll just go home."

I didn't understand about the card but I don't question her explanation. Instead I ask, "You'll keep your baby?"

"Yes."

I smile gratefully and send a quick "thank you" up to heaven.

Now really, what a flimsy excuse! Her card not right! "God, how did you manage that?"

"My ways are not your ways," God seems to answer.

Yes, if we sometimes are not able to help, God can use the clinic itself to achieve his purpose and save the baby.

God supplies and does what we cannot do. God just wants us to be there.

Notes

1. St. Thérèse of Lisieux, *Story of a Soul,* third ed., trans. John Clarke, OCD (Washington, DC: ICS Publications, 1996), 28.

2. Ibid., 27.

3. Rev. J. N. Grou, SJ, *The Characteristics of True Devotion,* ed. Rev. Samuel H. Frisbee, SJ (New York: Benziger Brothers, 1894), 39.

4. Ibid., 68–69.

5. Ibid., 182.

CHAPTER FOUR

Postabortion Help and Healing: From a River of Tears, a Rainbow Emerges

A study published in the May 13, 2003, *Canadian Medical Association Journal* stated that a review of the medical records of 56,741 California Medicaid patients revealed that women who had abortions were 2.6 times more likely than delivering women to be hospitalized for psychiatric treatment in the first 90 days following abortion or delivery.[1]

A woman is naturally sensitive and caring toward others. It is these qualities in women that help bring them out in men. An abortion is an unnatural act. When a woman has an abortion, she puts a wall up around her heart. She becomes desensitized as a way of surviving and avoiding the tears.

It is difficult for her friends and family to reach out to her. Maybe they were the rain dance that brought about this river of tears. Perhaps they were trying to help. Perhaps they were selfish.

This river of tears, this unnatural disaster, cannot be left alone. The river of tears flows through every town and village, sweeping away family life. Who will build the much needed dam to save civilization?

The Helpers of God's Precious Infants reach out to women who are suffering from their abortion experience. Sometimes the postabortive women and men seek out the Helpers knowing that the love they were shown on their way to having an abortion was genuine, and that these same Helpers who tried to prevent this tragedy will assist them now in their sorrow and regret.

The Helpers speak about God's love and forgiveness and make referrals to organizations such as Rachel's Helpers.

Dr. Florence Maloney has worked with postabortive women for many years. The following is a description of the program she runs, as well as a few testimonies from women who have found healing and peace.

Rachel's Helpers—A Pathway for Healing

Rachel's Helpers is an outreach program for women who have experienced an abortion of a child. Recognizing the deep emotional aftereffects of this experience, Rachel's Helpers moves to meet the woman in her need to talk about her feelings and to find internal peace.

The program utilizes *Forgiven and Set Free*,[2] a postabortion Bible study, by Linda Cochrane, that helps to guide the participants in recognizing that our wonderful God is ever present to comfort and strengthen all of us in our hardships and trials, and helps them to learn of God's tender, loving mercy.

Testimony from
Three Anonymous Witnesses

Journey to healing through
Project Rachel

Project Rachel is a national postabortion ministry that reaches out to those hurting emotionally and spiritually after involvement with abortion. Through Project Rachel, volunteers like me lead those who have experienced abortion on a healing journey from acceptance to forgiveness. Bridge to Life, a Rachel's Helpers Bible Study, is available to people of all faiths and denominations who are in need of healing.

Why is there a need for a postabortion ministry in the United States today? On January 22, 1973, when I was sixteen-years-old, the United States Supreme Court gave mothers the legal right to have their unborn baby killed, forcibly taken from inside them at any time until birth, at their request.

That decision by the U.S. Supreme Court affected all American citizens in some way, including you and me. To this date, over 40,000,000 babies have been killed through abortions in the United States alone, leaving millions of women and men emotionally and sometimes physically wounded and shattered from their abortion experiences.

The painful secret

Who am I? I am one of those millions of women and men who have experienced an abortion and Post-abortion Syndrome. At age nineteen, a sophomore in college, I became pregnant. I told my fiancé but no one else. I didn't tell my widowed mother, my sister, or my best friend. I didn't want anyone to know that I was sexually active or that I was pregnant. My fiancé chose to keep my pregnancy a secret and decided that we would handle the situation ourselves.

I rationalized that Rose, a college acquaintance of mine, had already had three abortions, and it was legal; it was no big deal. So I called one of the many advertised clinics and made a Saturday appointment to have a pregnancy test. I was told that I was seven weeks pregnant, and without serious thought, discussion, or counseling, I made an immediate decision to have a "suction aspiration procedure" performed on the following Saturday. The word *abortion* was not used to describe what I was to receive, and I was told that it would be a very "simple procedure."

I remember the location of the clinic, but I don't remember any details of the abortion itself. I don't even remember seeing a doctor or a nurse. My fiancé and I didn't talk about our experience during our short ride home, or any other day after that, nor to this day. I never told anyone else about it either until 1996, nineteen years later, when I spoke with a priest. I was convinced that my secret was safe and that no one else would ever know about it, and I would never have to think about it again. I buried the memory of being pregnant and having an abortion deep within myself, never expecting to have to recall it again. Little did I realize then that my secret was no secret to God. God knew what I had done because God had "knit my little one, formed my little one, before the foundation of time" (Jer 1:5). I didn't understand that I had only fooled myself.

A few days after I had graduated from college and nearly two years to the day of the abortion, something happened to me that I was unable to explain. Suddenly I felt extremely sad, and surprisingly I did not want to see my fiancé anymore. I refused his calls and visits and even returned a bouquet of long-stemmed red roses he had sent me, thinking he had done something to offend me. I was inconsolable. He was very confused by my actions. He and everyone else around me wanted to know what was wrong, but I was unable to tell them because I did not know what was happening myself. I just knew that I was experiencing deep emotional pain for which I had no explanation.

I returned my engagement ring to him, and I felt a sense of great relief. He was no longer my fiancé, but part of a painful memory that I had already erased.

After two years, I married another young man. Throughout my seventeen-year marriage, which ended in divorce two years ago, I was depressed, angry, and argumentative. I rarely smiled, and I preferred to be alone. Unknowingly, I had experienced the turbulent emotional after effect of abortion that I now know as Postabortion Syndrome.

About five years ago, my abortion experience began to surface through flashbacks and dreams, nineteen years after the abortion. It was a reality that I could no longer deny. It was painful, and it was real. I was devastated when I realized that I had intentionally killed my own flesh and blood—a baby that had begun to grow inside of me. My depression led me to consult a therapist. The therapist minimized my deep emotional pain and told me that abortion was not a big deal and that anyone in my situation would have done the same thing. Dissatisfied with her perspective, I made a decision to seek God's forgiveness in the sacrament of reconciliation.

After receiving the sacrament, my emotional pain, guilt, and shame didn't just evaporate. I continued to feel guilty, shameful, and unforgiven. I felt that I needed more help, but I didn't know where to turn because it seemed that no one understood the pain that I was feeling. I was desperate to talk with someone who would understand.

I called the Project Rachel hotline and spoke with a compassionate woman who listened to me and explained that what I was feeling was very common and was called "Postabortion Syndrome." Women, men, doctors, nurses, or anyone who experiences abortion directly or indirectly may suffer from PAS in some way. A person may experience some or many of these symptoms, including suicidal thoughts, guilt, prolonged grief, anxiety, memory loss, physical symptoms, lack of emotion, depression, sleep disturbances, alcohol or drug dependence, or the inability to form relationships. PAS symptoms may go on indefinitely unless a person takes steps to deal with the trauma in an effort to experience healing.

Is healing possible? I can tell you that healing is possible for postabortive women who seek help. I have personally experienced God's healing by participating in a Rachel's Helpers Bible study group. Our Bible study group met weekly for twelve weeks. Group members received the Bible study book *Forgiven and Set Free* without charge. We read assigned lessons and scriptural passages at home and then discussed them each week in a congenial small-group setting.

For the first time, I felt understood. I was heard, consoled, and guided. I was given an opportunity to work through my pain, guilt, and shame in the context of Scripture. I was able to accept that I am "forgiven and set free" according to God's grace. Through God's word I came to understand my emotions, accept what I had done, and experience healing. I can testify that God's word is true, according to Matthew 5:4: "Blessed are they who mourn, for they will be comforted." I thank God for his grace in healing me, the pastor of the church for providing the space for our group to meet, and the Bible study facilitators who selflessly volunteer their time to help others.

The impact of an abortion

Nobody tells you what it is like. At age seventeen, I was faced with a decision that would forever change my life. I thought an abortion would end my problems and worries. But instead it intensified them all.

July 26, 19___ is the day that I went ahead and followed a decision that I was not truly behind. Scared and young, I did not know what to do or whom to talk to. I remember going to the abortion clinic and feeling so bad and wanting to walk away—and thinking that, after it was done, my life would resume as planned.

Upon entering the actual room, my tears would not stop flowing. As they tied me down to the operating table, I remember them trying to get me to stop crying because if I didn't, I might not be able to breathe while under. I did not care. If I did not wake up, it was right for what I was doing to her. The last sight I saw as I fell asleep was the male doctor coming toward me. I was very upset that they did not tell me that the doctor was going to be a man, but I was so under that I could not do anything about it.

My postabortion experience was hard. Instantly I suffered for what I had done. Intense feelings of sadness, guilt, and shame all led to a deep depression that lasted well over a year. It made living daily life hard. I would cry constantly, so much so that I made myself weak. I would get sick, and I slept so much that I missed out on many things, including work and school. I never ate and would just stay home and stare at the wall and think about what I had done. I felt that life was not worthwhile anymore. Suicide was an idea; the pain of what I had done was overwhelming.

Life with my boyfriend was even harder. The majority of postabortion relationships end in breakup. We were determined to prove that wrong. But instead we realized why most don't work. We would constantly fight and say things that would hurt each other. We would always cross the line of respect. It is hard when two people love each other and go through something so emotional. It takes a lot to try to keep it together. Everyone mourns differently, which is okay, but how do you comfort someone that is mourning at the same time in a different manner? The fighting made my depression grow even stronger, and I did not think there was a way back.

Shortly after my experience, I found the phone number to Bridge to Life. Angry at why I could not have found it earlier, I took it as a sign. After numerous failed attempts, I finally got myself to call. That was the best thing I could have done. They extended their hand and love to me, without judging me. Not being judged was very important. They gave me the strength to pull my life together and learn from my mistakes.

I started seeing a great counselor who understood me and gave me the time and patience to open up. After a few sessions, I was so at ease. Talking to someone helped. My boyfriend even came every other session to try to deal with it, too. It helped us but not enough. We still separated.

An abortion is no quick fix; instead, it may be a start to something even worse. Although it affects everyone differently, what can happen can be devastating. I look at a baby and still think of mine and what she may have looked like. I have learned to live with what I have done, but the pain is still there, almost four years later. I am sure that it will be with me as long as I breathe. But I have turned all my emotions into a useful source. I now use my experience to help others, and the Lord has guided me into the career path I would like to pursue.

I view my little girl as my guardian angel. You can sometimes catch me talking to her. I try to make her proud of me, and I hope that when we meet she will forgive me and understand why I did what I did. Even if I can't have her physically with me, I feel her soul surrounding me and watching me. These feelings are something that I am very grateful to have.

Thank you for your forgiveness

"Praise the Lord, O my soul, and forget not all his benefits—who forgives all your sins and heals all your diseases, who redeems your life from the pit and crowns you with love and compassion" (Ps 103:2–4).

Father, my heart cries out with sorrow and regret for the sin I've committed. How can I possibly forgive myself for such a deed? I know you have already forgiven me, now help me to forgive myself.

Forgiving myself was the most difficult part of the healing journey. The feelings I had toward my abortions were dormant for thirteen years. I was twenty-five and twenty-eight when I made the decisions to terminate my pregnancies. Innately I knew what I was doing was wrong, but there just didn't seem to be any other way out. In my mind, I didn't think of abortion as ending the lives of my children but as the only solution to my problem. I was so afraid of being a single mother. As I began my healing, I realized I was more concerned with my reputation than the lives of my children. The thought of having to face the world, unmarried and alone, was terrifying.

The procedures were done in my gynecologist's office. The vacuum aspiration procedure took less than three minutes to suck the lives of my children from my womb. After each procedure, I sank deeper and deeper into an abyss. This was what my life was like for the next thirteen years. I was awake during both procedures, and they were extremely painful. During my last abortion, I must have been farther along in my pregnancy because it was more painful than my first. I remember asking my doctor why I was in such pain. He told me that my uterus was contracting; I was giving birth. After the abortion, as I lay on the table waiting to be taken into the recovery room, I looked down, and there in the little silver pan were the remains of my child. The pain in that memory goes beyond description, and it filled me with such remorse. I felt such an urgency to end my pregnancies because I didn't want to bond with my children-to-be for fear of changing my mind about what I felt I had to do. I didn't listen to the quiet voice telling me not to do it—that everything would work out fine. Now I know that voice was the voice of the Holy Spirit, whom God sent to be our Wonderful Counselor. Only I didn't listen to the Spirit's counsel.

As the years passed, alcohol became my refuge. It seemed to fill the void that aborting my children left in my heart. I began looking for love in all the wrong places with all the wrong men. I had such a sense of worthlessness. It seemed to me the only way to face another day was to numb myself with alcohol. I began having suicidal thoughts. My life became fruitless, hopeless, and useless. As far as I was concerned, there was no reason to continue living. I was in therapy for a while, but the counselors had no idea what was wrong with me. I became obsessed with the idea of death, wondering what it would feel like not to have to feel this never-ending pain anymore. The sad part is that I was oblivious as to why I was feeling this way. I didn't know that I was suffering from what is now known as postabortion syndrome. *Roe v. Wade* had set a precedent, making abortion legal. The terminations were done in the privacy of my gynecologist's exclusive office, not in some abortion clinic with people outside protesting. Why was my spirit tormenting me? I later learned that when a woman aborts her child, something happens on a deeper level of her consciousness. Psychologically, a price is paid. A life process is interrupted when an abortion takes place in a woman's body. Women were created by God to nurture and protect children.

I lived in denial for years and didn't even realize it. Through healing, I have learned that denial helps us to live with loss or trauma because the human psyche can only handle so much stress before it shuts down. Denial helps us to survive our immediate pain, but sooner or later we have to accept that we have suffered a loss, and with postabortive women, that we have caused the loss as well.

In 1989, I surrendered my life to Jesus Christ. He became my refuge. He pulled me out of the abyss. As my relationship with him became more intimate, he began to reveal the sins of my abortions to me. He sent me to my pastor, and I confessed to her that I had two abortions in my past. She prayed for me and embraced me with love and compassion. She became an important vessel in my healing. She assured me that as long as I had repented before God, I could walk in his forgiveness. Never once did she make me feel condemned, guilty, or ashamed. This was a very important ingredient in my healing process. Having a pastor that I was able to confide in and receive godly counsel from has been, and continues to be, a blessing in my life.

As my healing began, my pain intensified. I was in so much agony, my soul hurt. I had finally come to realize what I had done, that I was responsible for ending my children's lives. I had just lost my mom whom I loved so dearly. She was my dearest friend, and I was devastated over her death. But the pain over her death didn't compare to the agony I felt because of my abortions. The suicide thoughts became even more intense.

I thank God for his grace and mercy because God kept me forever in his care. God allowed me to realize the sin of my abortions *after* I surrendered my life to him. I believe God knew if I had not known his grace and mercy as a Christian, I would have taken my life. God allowed me to go through a postabortion Bible study where there was an atmosphere of love and acceptance in an environment where healing was able to take place. The "Group" allowed me to walk through my abortions step-by-step with other women who shared the same experiences.

Jesus has assured me that my children are in heaven with him. He has let me know that he has forgiven me, my children have forgiven me, and he has shown me how to forgive myself. Knowing this enables me to walk in freedom from guilt, shame, and condemnation. Jesus has allowed me to trade in my sorrows for his joy.

I cannot erase the many years I wasted on alcoholism, promiscuity, and shame. But I believe that God has given me a mandate to help other women and men who have experienced the pain of abortion to find healing and forgiveness in Jesus Christ, and to let women and men who are faced with a crisis pregnancy know of the alternatives to abortion. The Lord says that we should comfort others as he has comforted us. That is my heart's desire.

Notes

1. http://www.cmaj.ca/cgi/content/full/168/10/1253.
2. Linda Cochrane, *Forgiven and Set Free: A Post-Abortion Bible Study for Women* (Grand Rapids, MI: Baker Books, 1996).

Epilogue

From a Sidewalk Counselor to a Pray-er

I came to sidewalk counsel today.
I arrived early. All alone, I began to pray.
A woman in crisis, the rosary, now on pause.
I offer her help and support—Yes, it's a worthy cause.
But how can I find strength without the Creed?
Without prayer, it's just another good deed.

Like an angel you arrived, holding the key.
Rosary in hand, you answered my heartfelt plea.
You continued my rosary; I felt your strength build on
     mine.
I now work harder to save lives and souls, one at a
     time.
Because you are here praying, I know that is why—
I swallow my pride, and give it another try.

While many are shut in during this rainstorm, you have
     come out to dance.
Hearing Christ's call, you wanted life to have a fighting
     chance.

To go out into the rain is to have the courage and
   strength to speak
About Christ's Way, Truth, and Love, which those in
   the darkness seek.
But to bring Christ's Love to those who are drowning
   in the rain
(the unborn children, their parents, and the abortion
   mill gang)
is to dance in the rain with those of us still somewhat
   sane.

You dance in the rain, and every week you come back.
Distractions and temptations are not things that you
   lack.
Despite your weaknesses and search for support,
You continue to pray that their lives will not be cut
   short.
Thank you for sharing this gift from God with me
   today.
Together, we can make a difference, if only we pray!

The Dance of Salvation

Sometimes we may get tired of dancing in the rain
in front of the killing place. The abortion seekers put us
off, sometimes they lie, they stare past us and ignore us;
they may even, at times, stare at us and insult us. They
are drowning in the present culture, and those who hold
the truth and light of Christ offer life preservers of hope
and life. It requires patience, perseverance, prayer, and

love to get through the morning, to get through to them....

But then this refrain permeates the air and captures our hearts. It is the biblical James 5:19–20 who instructs us:

"My brothers (and sisters), the case may arise among you of someone straying from the truth and of another bringing him back. Remember this: the person who brings a sinner back from his way will save his soul from death and cancel a multitude of sins."

Who is such a person?

Those who pray and counsel outside the abortion mills fit this description.

James's lyrics are extraordinary in their meaning. Invigorating and exciting, their lively beat draws us to the dance—right there on the sidewalk amid all the rain. Now light on our feet, we are airborne. Our sins no longer weigh us down, for they have been canceled.

Our churches hold many social dances for diverse groups; for teens and singles, for charitable causes, and even for senior citizens. But the dance according to St. James transcends them all. It is the Dance of Salvation and of Eternal Life.

Each one of you is invited to attend.

Crisis Pregnancy and Postabortion Resources

National Hotlines will give local referrals.

America's Crisis Pregnancy Help Line	(800) 672-2296
Birthright	(800) 550-4900
Pregnancy Hotline	(800) 848-5683
Rachel's Helpers	(718) 939-6646

Rachel's Helpers is a sensitive, confidential postabortion reconciliation program that leads to reconciliation with oneself, the unborn child, one's family, the church, and God. In a caring and hopeful context, participants receive help from specially trained counselors and psychologists to help process their feelings and deal with unresolved conflicts.

Project Rachel:
    1-800-5WE-CARE (National Referral Line)
    Website: http://home.catholicweb.com/projectrachel/

This diocesan-based postabortion healing ministry, founded in 1984 in the Archdiocese of Milwaukee by

Vicki Thorn, is composed of a network of specially trained clergy, spiritual directors, and therapists who provide skilled compassionate and confidential care to persons suffering from the aftereffects of abortion. While an outreach of the Catholic Church, Project Rachel is open to anyone who struggles with an abortion loss, including women, men, parents, grandparents, siblings, friends, and others.

Carenet
101 W. Broad St., #500
Falls Church, VA 22046
(800) 395-HELP

Elliot Institute
P.O. Box 7348
Springfield, IL 62791-7348
(217) 535-8202
www.afterabortion.org

Healing Visions Network
National Youth Pro-Life Coalition
Jackson Avenue
Hastings on Hudson, NY 10706
(914) 478-0103

Heartbeat International
665 E. Dublin-Granville Road, Suite 440
Columbus, OH 43229
(888) 550-7577
http://www.heartbeatinternational.org/

Priests for Life
P.O. Box 141172
Staten Island, NY 10314
(888) PFL-3448, (718) 980-4400
www.priestsforlife.org

The Nurturing Network
P.O. Box 1489
White Salmon, WA 98672
(800) TNN-4MOM
http://www.nurturingnetwork.org/

Books

Cochrane, Linda. *Forgiven and Set Free: A Post-Abortion Bible Study for Women.* Grand Rapids, MI: Baker Books, 1996.

Dillon, John J. *A Path to Hope: For Parents of Aborted Children and Those Who Minister to Them.* Mineola, NY: Resurrection Press, 1990.

Hayford, Jack. *I'll Hold You in Heaven.* Ventura, CA: Regal Books from Gospel Light, 1986, 1990.

Mannion, Michael T. *Abortion and Healing: A Cry to Be Whole.* Kansas City, MO: Sheed and Ward, 1986.

Reardon, David. *Aborted Women: Silent No More.* Chicago, IL: Loyola University Press, 1987.

Reardon, David. *Making Abortion Rare.* Springfield, IL: Acorn Books, 1996.

Selby, Terry, and Marc Bockmon. *The Morning After: Help for Post-Abortion Syndrome.* Grand Rapids, MI: Baker Book House, 1990.